Gardening

Level 6 – Orange

Helpful Hints for Reading at Home

The graphemes (written letters) and phonemes (units of sound) used throughout this series are aligned with Letters and Sounds. This offers a consistent approach to learning, whether reading at home or in the classroom.

HERE IS A LIST OF PHONEMES FOR THIS PHASE OF LEARNING. AN EXAMPLE OF THE PRONUNCIATION CAN BE FOUND IN BRACKETS.

Phase 5			
ay (day)	ou (out)	ie (tie)	ea (eat)
oy (boy)	ir (girl)	ue (blue)	aw (saw)
wh (when)	ph (photo)	ew (new)	oe (toe)
au (Paul)	a_e (make)	e_e (these)	i_e (like)
o_e (home)	u_e (rule, cube)		

Phase 5 Alternative Pronunciations of Graphemes			
a (hat, what)	e (bed, she)	i (fin, find)	o (hot, so, other)
u (but, unit)	c (cat, cent)	g (got, giant)	ow (cow, blow)
ie (tied, field)	ea (eat, bread)	er (farmer, herb)	ch (chin, school, chef)
y (yes, by, very)	ou (out, shoulder, could, you)		

HERE ARE SOME WORDS WHICH YOUR CHILD MAY FIND TRICKY.

Phase 5 Tricky Words			
oh	their	people	Mr
Mrs	looked	called	asked
could			

TOP TIPS FOR HELPING YOUR CHILD TO READ:

- Allow children time to break down unfamiliar words into units of sound and then encourage children to string these sounds together to create the word.

- Encourage your child to point out any focus phonics when they are used.

- Read through the book more than once to grow confidence.

- Ask simple questions about the text to assess understanding.

- Encourage children to use illustrations as prompts.

This book focuses on /o_e/ and /oe/ and is an Orange level 6 book band.

Can you work out which of these pictures have names with o_e in them?

Answers: home, drone, stone, bone, robe

There are lots of parts to a gardening job. Gardeners need to make sure that all the plants in a garden are looked after.

Gardeners may travel to big public gardens to do their jobs. Some may travel to little gardens at peoples' homes.

When it is hot, gardeners check that each plant gets the right amount to drink. They may get out a hose or a can to help.

It is best for gardeners to spray close to the stem. This means that it all goes right to the roots.

Stem

Some gardens have a problem with weeds and stones. They can choke the plants that are supposed to be growing there.

Gardeners can use a hoe to help them pull up weeds in the soil. Some hoes have a long pole so that people do not have to stoop as low.

Hoe

If a garden has too much grass, it will need to be mowed. Flat gardens are better to cut, as cutting on a slope can be hard.

Gardeners need to take care that they do not get hurt. They cannot let their toes near the sharp parts of the mower.

Sharp

Gardeners check that plants are not sick. If they are, gardeners work out how to make those plants better.

Some plants get attacked by bugs. Gardeners might have to spray them to keep the bugs off.

Bugs on a rose bud

Gardeners do not just look after adult plants. They may plant new ones, too. First, they poke a hole in some soil.

Then, they drop a seed in the hole and get it wet. They let the pot sit in the sunlight. Soon, a new plant springs up!

©2023 **BookLife Publishing Ltd.**
King's Lynn, Norfolk, PE30 4LS, UK

ISBN 978-1-80505-078-0

All rights reserved. Printed in China.
A catalogue record for this book is
available from the British Library.

Gardening
Written by Charis Mather
Designed by Isabella Croker

An Introduction to BookLife Readers...

Our Readers have been specifically created in line with the London Institute of Education's approach to book banding and are phonetically decodable and ordered to support each phase of the Letters and Sounds document.

Each book has been created to provide the best possible reading and learning experience. Our aim is to share our love of books with children, providing both emerging readers and prolific page-turners with beautiful books that are guaranteed to provoke interest and learning, regardless of ability.

BOOK BAND GRADED using the Institute of Education's approach to levelling.

PHONETICALLY DECODABLE supporting each phase of Letters and Sounds.

EXERCISES AND QUESTIONS to offer reinforcement and to ascertain comprehension.

CLEAR DESIGN to inspire and provoke engagement, providing the reader with clear visual representations of each non-fiction topic.

AUTHOR INSIGHT:
CHARIS MATHER

Charis Mather is a children's author at BookLife Publishing who has a love for reading and writing. Her studies in linguistics and experiences working with young readers have given her a knack for writing material that suits a range of ages and skill levels. Charis is passionate about producing books that emphasise the fun in reading and is convinced that no matter how much you already know, there is always something new to learn.

PHASE 5 /o_e/ /oe/

This book focuses on /o_e/ and /oe/ and is an Orange level 6 book band.

Image Credits Images are courtesy of Shutterstock.com. With thanks to Getty Images, Thinkstock Photo and iStockphoto. Cover – pernsanitfoto, Pixel-Shot, Anconer Design, K N. p2–3 – LesPalenik, Tarzhanova, Svetlana Serebryakova, VIEWVEAR, PROFFIPhoto, BCFC, khunkornStudio, ruzanna. p4–5 – michaeljung, Serhii Bobyk. p6–7 – amedeoemaja, Aleksandar Malivuk. p8–9 – Lost_in_the_Midwest, Jon Rehg. p10–11 – Artith chotitayangkoon, Virrage Images. p12–13 – VH-studio, Miguel Angel RM, CandyRetriever. p14–15 – dasytnik, Sentelia.